I AM HIP HOP

Book Series

Easy A.D. of the Legendary Cold Crush Brothers

Volume I

By
Easy A.D.
&
Charles Taylor Jr.

Cover Art & Illustrations
By
Anthony Riley

About US

About the Authors & Illustrator
Easy A.D. (Author)

Easy A.D. is the heart and soul behind this book series! Not only is he a co-author, but he's also the star of the first book – talk about bringing a story to life! As a co-founding member of the Legendary Cold Crush Brothers, Easy A.D. is a hip hop icon who has rocked the mic and excited crowds for decades.

From his roots in the South Bronx, Easy A.D. always had a passion for music and sports. He and the Cold Crush Brothers helped shape hip hop culture in New York City, across the U.S., and around the world. They blazed a trail for generations of artists to follow.

These days, you'll find Easy A.D. still performing, still pushing hip hop forward through his various businesses, and – get this – working with public schools to encourage healthy living and boost reading skills in kids of color. He's living proof that dreams come true. And now, he's dedicated to helping other kids achieve their dreams too.

Charles Taylor (Co-author)
Charles is a writer who's deeply connected to his community. He's all about telling the stories of those working to make a difference in New York City's neighborhoods. He's passionate about social justice and uses his writing to shine a light on the struggles and triumphs of communities of color facing gentrification.

Over the years, Charles has teamed up with artists and organizations to use art as a tool for positive change. He's written countless articles, grant proposals, and even produced videos to bring attention to important issues like inequality and marginalization.

Charles has an incredible knack for bringing people together and finding common ground. He's a tireless advocate for those who need a voice and believes in the power of art to create a more just and equitable world.

Anthony Riley (Illustrator)
Anthony Riley is the artistic genius who brought the first book in this series to life with his vibrant illustrations. He's known for capturing the essence of hip hop culture in his work.

Anthony's illustrations in the book are a throwback to his iconic flyer designs from the 70s and 80s – back when hip hop was just taking off, and flyers were the way to spread the word! His art adds an authentic touch and visual energy to the story, taking you right back to those early days of hip hop.

Copyright

For my mother, Jean Gilchrist Harris,
my father, Frank Hezekiah Harris——A.D.

Copyright © 2025 by Easy A.D.
All rights reserved.
Self-published by Easy A.D.
ISBN:979-8-989-8679-0-5

No portion of this book may be reproduced in any form without written permission from the publisher or author, except as permitted by U.S. copyright law.

For Information, contact, easyad@iamhiphopbookseries.com

Preface

Easy A.D. here, from the Legendary Cold Crush Brothers!

I'm super excited to introduce my I Am Hip Hop Children's Book Series. This project is my way of sharing the real stories of hip hop with you. I've been there since the beginning, rocking the mic and watching this culture grow. I've met so many amazing people along the way. Some are big names you already know, and some are hidden figures who deserve their shine. Every single one of them helped build hip hop into what it is today.

These books are gonna take you on a journey through hip hop culture. We're talking personal interviews, rare photos, the whole nine yards. I want you to feel like you're right there with me and my brothers back in the day, discovering the power of hip hop. I remember when I was a kid, just starting out. We used to go to shows in the park, watching our heroes rock the crowd. Man, we were blown away! Years later, I found myself on stage, looking out at a sea of faces. Some of those kids went on to become legends themselves! They told me how much those shows inspired them, and that's exactly what I want these books to do for you. These are stories of real people who chased their dreams and made history. I hope they inspire you to do the same. And when you reach the top of your chosen field, don't forget to reach back and help the next generation rise. That's how we keep hip hop alive!

Peace and Honor, Easy A.D.

Introduction

I Am Hip Hop

Young readers! Get ready to drop some beats and learn some serious knowledge! Ever wonder where your favorite music, fly styles, and awesome rhymes came from? Well, guess what? Easy A.D., a real-deal pioneer from the Legendary Cold Crush Brothers, is gonna take you way back to the old school!

Boom! "I Am Hip Hop" is a brand new book series created by Easy A.D. himself. It's bursting with stories about all the DJs, MCs, graffiti artists, and dancers, and others who first brought hip hop to life. You'll discover the big names and the unsung heroes who helped turn hip hop into the global phenomenon it is today.

In the first book, we're dropping the mic on Easy A.D. and the Cold Crush Brothers! Follow their incredible journey from the streets of the Bronx to rocking stages worldwide. It's a story about creativity, passion, and how music can change the world.

Get ready to connect the dots between the past and present of hip hop! With "I Am Hip Hop," you'll see how the music, fashion, language, and media you dig today have roots that go way back. It's an exciting adventure that will have you shouting, "I am Hip Hop!"

Table of Contents

Foreword : To my Hip Hop family, past, present, and future............1

Chapter 1 : Family Life 3

Chapter 2 : B-Ball Rules 11

Chapter 3 : Time to Rhyme 25

Chapter 4 : Cold Crush Origins..33

Chapter 5 : Battle for Hip Hop Supremacy 41

Chapter 6 : Elements - Wild Style Movie......................................47

Chapter 7 : From Cassette Tapes to Records................................59

Featured Track : Freestyle 63

Epilogue : A Message From A.D. 65

Acknowledgments..67

Foreword

To my Hip Hop family, past, present, and future

The words "I AM" are the ultimate power move. They echo through every corner of the universe, from sacred temples to the streets we grew up on. To say "I AM" is to own your truth, no matter what the world throws at you. That's the essence of Hip Hop, isn't it? To be yourself, unapologetically. To move to your own beat, even when everyone else is trying to tell you how to dance. Easy A.D. is the embodiment of that spirit. When he declares "I AM Hip Hop," it's not just a boast—it's a battle cry for our culture. He's been holding it down since day one, from the streets of NYC to rocking stages with the Legendary Cold Crush Brothers. He's the guy who said, "I don't need to get high to be fly." He walked his own path, never compromising who he was.

This ain't some fairytale, though. Easy A.D. faced the same struggles, the same demons we all did. But he made it through, stronger than ever. And he didn't need anything but his own strength to get there. That's a lesson for all of us. He's not just a legend for what he did. He's a legend for who he IS. The dude rolls with Tony Tone, Caz, JDL, The Almighty KG, and Charlie Chase! He's in the room with the game changers.

So when Easy A.D. says "I AM Hip Hop," you better believe it's the truth. And now he's sharing that truth with the next generation. His children's book series will take you deep into the heart of our culture, from DJing to breakdancing, from icons you know to the unsung heroes.

These are stories told by a true Hip Hop God, as Chuck D would say. So open your ears, open your minds, and let Easy A.D. school you on what it truly means to be Hip Hop.

DMC from Run-DMC

Chapter 1

Family Life

It was 1970, and the Bronx was burning. People were setting fires across the community. Families and city officials were upset. Parents worried about keeping their kids and homes safe. It was scary, because the fires could start anywhere without warning. The fires made many families and their children a little nervous and more careful. People kept going to work and school, and kept grocery shopping and walking their dogs. Whenever there was a fire, someone would run to the corner and pull the lever on a red fire box that sent an emergency signal to the New York City fire department.

A.D. Harris was born on a cool, clear morning at 5:44 a.m. on September 10 th at Fordham Hospital in the Bronx. His birth certificate wasn't picked up until September 13th, because it took a few days for his parents to decide on his name. Adrian had such long hair that people sometimes mistook him for a cute little girl. As the newest addition to the family, Adrian received lots of love and attention from his parents and older sisters. He was a very happy baby.

Adrian, who was soon to be known to all as Easy A.D., was a smart, curious, and active left-handed Virgo. He loved living in the South Bronx. It was the most beautiful place in the whole world. He could close his eyes wherever he was and almost taste one of his mom's delicious meals. He yearned for his favorite: fresh, yummy hamburger patties and soft, tasty hamburger buns with slices of Kraft melted cheese and a side of hot, crispy french fries. It was always a treat when his mom bought the buns instead of Wonder white bread.

Dinner at A.D.'s house anytime was his favorite surprise. Would it be the fat Italian sausages that swelled like tasty mountains in boiling water? Or would it be the best meal anyone ever had—spaghetti with a few scoops of applesauce? That's right, applesauce on the side. Now, that's the kind of meal A.D. could eat every day.

Eating-and eating together-was very important for A.D.'s family. They had a big dining table with an extension in the middle to make it longer. The table had room for A.D., his parents, and his seven sisters. It was a fun family time to eat together. A.D. loved his family very much and enjoyed all the time he spent with them. He was the fourth child and only boy. After homework, the family got together to have fun and eat dinner after a full day.

Easy A.D. eating breakfast with his seven sisters Sherry, Cynthia, Regina, Jeanette, Daphne, Denise and Wanda.

The family had two bathrooms and two kitchens. One kitchen was used as a storage space. A.D. always had his own room, so he had plenty of space. A.D.'s mother woke up before everyone so that she could get ready first. A.D.'s mother was great at organizing the family's home. She made sure that everyone had everything they needed to enjoy themselves, and make good choices in life. Something that she did was a mystery to A.D.

One day, when A.D. was 10 years old, he asked his mom to let him help her shop at the local supermarket. He was very curious and wanted to learn how to shop for food. Every week, his mom would leave the house and, a little later, magically reappear at the door with lots of groceries. If he went shopping too, he might be able to get some of the goodies that he liked best. A.D.'s mom always took two shopping carts to the supermarket because she shopped for such a large family. He followed his mom around the store as they filled up both baskets. The mystery was finally solved. A.D. learned that grocery shopping was serious work, and he was happy that he could help.

A.D.'s family was on public assistance - something he didn't know much about. What he did know was his family always had what they needed, even though there were so many of them. Christmas and Easter were very important times for A.D.'s family and community. He and his sisters loved Christmas, because it was when everyone got new clothing—sneakers, t-shirts, underwear, socks, gloves, and hats. It was always a very big deal. A.D. also loved to get new toys like Hot Wheels, a garbage truck, an electric football, and a chemistry set. Toys were cool, but clothes were better.

Easy A.D. playing his drum set on Christmas Day

One Christmas when he was in elementary school, A.D.'s mom asked him what he wanted for Christmas. He said he wanted a drum set. This was something he'd thought about for a long time. On Christmas Eve, he was hanging out in the living room with some of his sisters. His older sisters, Sherry and Cynthia, came in the front door with some shopping bags and went straight to their mother's bedroom and closed the door. Around 2 a.m., A.D. heard his sister's boyfriend playing the drums. The next morning, A.D. hugged his mom and told her how happy he was to get the wonderful drum set. A.D. began drumming every chance he got—mornings, afternoons, nights, weekdays, and weekends. He soon realized he had to slow down and only play the drums when it wouldn't disturb others. He was a fast learner and improved quickly.

Every morning before school, A.D. and his sisters gathered round the dining table for their mother's breakfast masterpiece. Most mornings, they would all eat a big bowl of oatmeal with a heap of Domino's sugar and lots of butter. Sometimes they had a stack of thick pancakes made with Aunt Jemima Pancake Mix, with buttermilk syrup, real butter, milk, and Domino's sugar. Of course there was always Nestle Quik to make chocolate milk. They also had the tastiest eggs and sausage in the world. It was a great way to start the day.

A.D. was always anxious to get to school. He did lots of fun things with his classmates and had some very nice teachers. Every morning, he and his sisters would get up early, get ready quickly, and get off to school on time. Their mom made sure there were no slip-ups. P.S. 157 was the place to be. A.D. had some really amazing teachers and did some exciting things. His third grade teacher, Ms. Webster, taught the class how to fold The New York Times, even though they were too young to read it at the time. They were preparing for the future.

Ms. Chamberlain, A.D.'s fourth grade teacher, at PS 50, a different school, had a great merit and demerit system. Students who did good class work could earn points to be used to buy cool stuff from a table in the front of the classroom. The table held all kinds of goodies including candy, games, books, and baseball cards. A.D. asked the other kids not to take the baseball cards, and they agreed. The packs of cards were not the regular ten-pack. Instead, each pack had ten ten-packs for a total of one hundred cards. It was almost too good to be true. A.D. worked hard for the merits and wound up getting more cards than anyone he knew.

The school sometimes had special guests like Manhattan Borough President Percy Sutton and the greatest soccer star ever, Pele from Brazil. School was like an adventure. A.D. learned exciting new things and gained new skills in class.

The teachers had very different lessons to teach the students, but they had one important thing in common. They all talked to the students in warm and caring tones. They were patient and interested in the students' lives. This is what A.D. loved most of all about school. It's what motivated him to try new things and always do his best.

A.D. loved music and sports and had lots of fun times with his sisters. Things were going fine until something sad happened. Someone set a fire in one of the apartments on an upper floor in his building. A.D.'s family lived on the second floor. They had to evacuate the building like a fire drill at school. The firemen saved all the tenants and quickly put the fire out, but it was too late to save the building. The firemen's hoses flooded most apartments which couldn't be used anymore. The building had been destroyed by fire and water damage. 890 Eagle Avenue would no longer be their home. It was an unhappy day for everyone who lived in the building, but it was the beginning of a new adventure.

Chapter 2

B-Ball Rules

After the fire, the Red Cross worker and the fire department chief talked to all the families about moving.

Easy A.D. and his family watch the firemen try to put out the fire.

The Harris family was moved to the elegant Grand Concourse Hotel in the South Bronx. The spacious hotel made A.D. feel important. The staff members were friendly and helpful.

Every area of the hotel was sparkling clean with a fresh aroma. A.D.'s family stayed on the eleventh floor, which looked out over the magnificent Grand Concourse. Down the hill, they could clearly see the greatest stadium in the world, Yankee Stadium. They had a once-in-a-lifetime chance to see the world champion New York Yankees baseball team and the New York Giants football team play games from their window. It wasn't the same as their own home, but they were happy to be together. They stayed at the hotel for a couple of weeks, and then the Red Cross worker told them that he had found them a wonderful new apartment. The Grand Concourse Hotel was a fantastic experience to remember, but it was time for the Harris family to move on. Soon, A.D. and his family moved from the Grand Concourse Hotel to an apartment building at 1471 Vyse Avenue off 172nd Street. They lived at the top of a big hill. It was a long walk to go up the hill, and a long walk to go down. A.D. and his sisters were super excited about their new apartment. Their apartment was spacious enough to accommodate A.D.'s large family. The landlord made a new doorway between two apartments to create one very large living space. The new apartment had two living rooms, two bathrooms, and two kitchens. One of the kitchens was used as a storage space. It was an amazing place that Mrs. Harris soon made feel like home. A.D. met his neighbor and first friend, Adrian Fogg, at the new building. It was so cool that they were both named Adrian. They hung out a lot and talked about all kinds of things. They played with Army soldiers, watched sports on TV, and traded baseball cards. Adrian had a younger brother named Lionel and an older brother named Dennis. He also had two sisters named Rita and Martha.

Easy A.D. chills with his childhood friend, Adrian Fogg.

A.D. and Adrian liked to hang out munching on Pringles and playing around. Dennis taught the boys how to stretch and make some martial arts moves like Bruce Lee. After relocating, A.D. had to change schools. He went from PS 157 to CS 50 Clara Barton, which was a block and a half from A.D.'s new home. He went to the fourth grade soon after the school year began. At first, A.D. felt very uncomfortable in his new class and with his classmates. When he got there, the whole school was feeling sad about a gym teacher who had passed away of an aneurysm. A.D.'s teacher had the students put their heads down on their desks for some quiet time to deal with their feelings about the loss of their gym teacher. A.D. wasn't sure what he should do since he hadn't known the teacher. After a while, A.D. got comfortable in the new school with the students and teachers.

A.D. soon joined the Glee Club and participated in band. They were both led by a teacher named Ms. Glass. A.D. played the trumpet, bongos, congas, drums, tambourine, and maracas. This was A.D.'s first experience with instruments in a school setting. He also learned how to read music. A.D. soon began going to the after-school program. It was run by a teacher named Mr. Gollin from 4 p.m. to 6 p.m. Monday to Friday. A community worker named Elliot Tillman was asked to join the staff. He knew a lot about the community and how to keep kids safe. The after school program had many fun activities. He played lots of basketball, kickball, softball, floor hockey, and off-the-wall. He also did lots of arts and crafts projects. Soon, the school began a softball tournament where classes got together and formed teams to play against each other at lunchtime. In the after-school program, the teams worked on building their skills. At the end of the year, during an assembly in the auditorium at the school, A.D. was given a softball trophy for being the most valuable player in his grade. This was a very big deal for A.D. It was the first trophy that he had ever received, and he was very proud. Mr. Golin and Mr. Tillman got permission from A.D.'s parents to go to the 1665 Hoe Avenue Boys and Girls Club every day when the after school program was finished. This is where A.D. became a more competitive basketball player because he loved the game so much. The Boys and Girls Club membership card only cost one dollar a year, but it was worth a lot more. A.D. and his parents were happy about the low cost of the membership and all of the exciting activities that the club offered.

The Boys and Girls Club was open seven days a week with exciting games, great music, and good friends. A.D.'s days were full, and he didn't have time for anything else. A.D. went to school in the morning. Then he went to the after school program. Later in the day he would go to the Hoe Avenue Boys and Girls Club. There were so many things to do at the Boys and Girls Club, but before they started playing, everyone was required to do their homework. After homework was done, the kids were given a tasty snack. A.D. would have fun shooting hoops, boxing, playing floor hockey, bumper pool or board games, and hanging with his friends. A.D. usually got home around 9:30 or 10 p.m. Together, the Hoe Avenue Boys and Girls Club, the New York City police department, and CS 50 Clara Barton developed a program called Learn to Swim. The Learn to Swim program instructors were detectives from the 44th Precinct. It was a program for young students who couldn't afford expensive private swim lessons and didn't have many pools in their community. Every Thursday, right after lunchtime, A.D. and his class would leave the school and walk around the corner to the Boys and Girls Club for their weekly swimming lesson. When it was over, he would stay until the program closed like he always did.

John Isaacs was always at the door of the Boys Club checking the kids in. He would give the kids a lecture about life every day in his deep and pleasant voice. He made kids want to listen to him. He was a Boys Club hero, a basketball pioneer, and a community legend. A.D. loved to hear Mr. Isaacs talk about how important it was for everyone to take care of their community and each other. Mr. Isaacs reminded the kids to always do the best they could to help people who looked like them. A.D. never forgot his words.

A.D. made many friends and learned lots of fun things at the Boys Club. They had an awards dinner for everything. There were awards dinners for karate, basketball, gymnastics, swimming, boxing, and other activities. A.D. went to his first awards dinner while he was still in the fourth grade. There was a teen named Bobby Willis who received eighteen awards. A.D. promised himself that he would win athlete of the year, just like Bobby.

A.D. started working with an instructor named Jessie Cooper in the arts and crafts room. The Boys Club bought lots of shirts for different teams and activities. Jessie's job was to use special equipment to put numbers on the shirts. A.D. was very excited to learn the process by himself. One day, A.D. entered a contest to make a design about Africa out of any kind of material.

He made a really cool crown from a cardboard box and painted it bright colors. He looked forward to going to the awards dinner and maybe even winning an award.

Easy A.D. getting ready to play basketball at the Hoe Avenue Boys and Girls Club in the South Bronx

Unfortunately, A.D. never made it to the awards dinner. He was hurt in an accident the day of the event. A man ran into him with a bike and broke his ankle in the schoolyard during lunch period. The man didn't have permission to ride his bike in the schoolyard. He accidentally hit A.D. as the school staff chased him off school grounds. Even though he couldn't attend the event, A.D. won third prize. It was his first award. He was so proud to have won a Boys Club keychain for the African crown he created. The fifth grade was lots of fun and excitement. The days were filled with new things to do in school, and lots of basketball and good music after school. Elliot Tillman put together a basketball team that was part of the Boys Club basketball association. All of the different Boys Clubs around the city played against each other. A.D.'s team played against the Kips Bay Boys Club, the Columbus Boys Club, the Gramercy Boys Club, and many others. A.D. was ten years old and played in the eleven and under program. In his first year on the team, A.D. averaged ten points. The next year, he averaged twenty-seven points and ten assists. His hard work at practice and good teamwork made him a superstar. A.D. loved to win and didn't like to lose. He played hard, but he also had lots of fun. One day, in the summer after graduating from the sixth grade, a fire in an upstairs apartment forced all of the tenants to leave the building immediately. Once again, A.D.'s family safely escaped from their second-floor apartment. Luckily, no one was hurt in the fire.

The building was seriously damaged by the fire and water damage and had to be closed. The Harris family and their belongings moved to another hotel on 103rd Street and Broadway in Manhattan. Coincidently, they were placed on the eleventh floor again. A.D. and his family were very sad to leave their comfortable apartment at 1471 Vyse Avenue. The good thing was that they could always make a new home, as long as they had each other. On a hot August night, the Harris family moved from the hotel on 103rd Street and Broadway to 1460 Washington Avenue in the Claremont housing projects on the 12th floor. A.D. wasn't sure why, but he didn't enjoy living in the building. He had his own room but decided to sleep on the floor in front of his room. After a while, A.D. got used to the apartment, slept in his room, and finally settled into his new neighborhood. One evening, after leaving the Boys Club, A.D. stood outside talking with his friends before heading home. They started walking towards 173rd Street to buy something to eat. Back then, everything was more affordable. A slice of pizza and a soda cost thirty-five cents, or fifty cents if you wanted a topping. As A.D. and the guys were walking towards the pizza shop around 9 pm, and all of a sudden the lights went out everywhere. It was the first blackout that A.D. had ever experienced.

In the blackout, all of the storefronts and apartment buildings went dark in every direction. A.D. and his friends were slowly walking in the dark towards a popular clothing store on the corner. It sold sneakers, jeans, basketballs, and other sporting goods. Suddenly, a group of people ran past A.D. and his friends. Together, the group of people lifted up the gate at the entrance of the store and broke open the front door. They began grabbing as many coats, sneakers, and jeans as they could carry.
They stole almost everything from the store.

This scene depicts the blackout when all the lights went out in New York City.

A.D. and his friends stood on the sidewalk in shock. A.D. didn't dare take anything from the store. He knew that his mother wouldn't allow any stolen goods in his house. Some of A.D.'s friends lived in the Lambert projects on 180th Street and East Tremont Avenue. A couple of his friends lived close to the Boys Club. A.D. lived in the other direction on Washington Avenue. A.D. decided to walk home alone, so he said goodbye to his friends. He walked up Boston Road and through Crotona Park on the way home.

This scene shows people looting during the blackout in New York City.

There was a large supermarket near the exit to the park. In the dark, A.D. could make out lots of people carrying bags and pushing shopping carts full of food and other items from the market. They were excited and in a big hurry to take as much as possible and get out fast. It was amazing that all of the action was taking place in the dark. After most of the crowd had gone, A.D. stepped inside the market for a moment. He quickly took one Hershey candy bar to eat before he got upstairs to his apartment. Then A.D. slowly made his way home in the dark.

Early the next morning, everyone in A.D's building learned about a problem caused by the blackout. The water was turned off in the building and the tenants couldn't use their sinks, tubs, or toilets. Everyone had to take buckets and go downstairs to fill them up at a nearby fire hydrant. Then they had to carry the heavy buckets filled with water upstairs. A.D. and his family had to go up and down twelve flights of stairs. It was very hard work, but they had to do it.

Later in the week, A.D. noticed some changes in the neighborhood. Many of the stores in the main shopping area on Fordham Road had been broken into during the blackout. Some of the stores were boarded up, and others were being repaired by workers. People had stolen food, clothing, bicycles, mopeds, turntables, speakers, amplifiers, and anything else they could find. After the blackout, there were a lot of new DJs showing off their equipment and working on their skills. Soon, things went back to normal, but the blackout was something that A.D. would never forget. He was excited by the new music that was being made all across the neighborhood.

During the summer before middle school, A.D. played a lot of basketball. He played in the TIP basketball tournament, the Rucker Tournament, and a few other tournaments. He loved playing basketball more than anything, but he wanted have a new adventure.

One day, A.D. decided to go to a New York Mets game by himself. He made a plan to get the money and directions he needed for his big adventure. First, A.D. got a free subway map and figured out the train route to Shea Stadium in Flushing, Queens. He had saved enough money for his trip from an internship at the Boys and Girls Club. A.D. helped out daily in the locker room and received a small stipend every week. The chance to earn money as a twelve-year-old gave A.D. a new kind of confidence. He bought himself a new black and white TV. He was very careful about how he spent his money. For the baseball trip, A.D. bought himself a new right-handed first baseman's glove. It was the same glove worn by Ron Milner, the New York Mets' very popular first baseman. A.D. had money for carfare, a ticket to the game, and plenty of refreshments. A.D. was comfortable traveling anywhere by himself. He didn't like to travel with a bunch of other kids because he liked to make his own decisions. A.D. had learned that sometimes a few kids in a group could make bad decisions that got everyone in the group in trouble. A.D. was ready for his big adventure. He took the number seven train to the Shea Stadium station in Queens. He got on line and paid $11 for his ticket. Then, he walked to his seat in row number eleven. He was ready to see the first baseball game on his own. He was sitting next to a white family with a mom, dad, and two sons. The mom kept asking A.D. who he was with and if he wanted some food. She seemed to be worried about him being there without a grown-up. A.D. thanked the lady and asked her not to worry about him. He said that he was fine by himself and was trying to catch a baseball if a foul ball was hit near him. A.D. couldn't stop smiling and looking around the stands and the field. He was glad to be at the game. He bought a frankfurter, Cracker Jacks, a soda, and ice cream. As the game was about to start, A.D. looked around the stadium at all the people. He felt a sense of satisfaction. Now, it was time for someone to throw out the first pitch and to hear the umpire shout, "Play ball!" A.D.'s best friend, Donald Lamont, became his first MC partner. Rashid and his wife Stephanie worked at the Boys Club and were also DJs. Rashid taught Stephanie to be a DJ. They joined with A.D., Donald, and Frank Nitti to form a group called the Asalaam Brothers. 'Asalaam' means 'peace to you' in Arabic.

Easy A.D. rocking the mic with Donald D, his first MC partner

A.D.'s beginning in hip hop culture started at the Boys Club. He continued to go there every day after school. His mom and dad always supported him. They made sure that his dinner was still warm in the oven when he came home every night close to bedtime. Now, he was beginning to make a connection between basketball and rap music.

Chapter 3

Time to Rhyme

The Asalaam Brothers started doing house parties around the community. Donald D and A.D. wrote lots of rhymes and tried them out with different audiences. They were excited to play the Boys Club and the Lambert Center, where they got lots of love for their music. One day Rashid booked the group to play at the Sparkle. This was a very big deal, because usually groups with a big name that could draw a crowd were booked there. The Asalaam Brothers' members were excited and ready to perform when they got the bad news. The Sparkle burned down the week of their performance date. The group was disappointed, but they didn't let it stop them. They kept on doing community parties and working to make better music. Donald D and A.D. kept busy doing their thing at the Boys Club. They played basketball, flag football, floor hockey, and tennis. They also worked hard on improving their MC skills. People from different groups began to come to their performances. They were starting to get a buzz in the community. This helped build their confidence. Then they did something very exciting. They bought sweatshirts with their group's name on the front—the Asalaam Brothers—and each of their names on the back. The sweatshirts were dark blue with white letters, and they were so cool. This was the way that people in hip hop culture branded the names of things. It was the thing to do. A.D. and his crew always wore the most stylish hip hop fashion. They wore Lee jeans with lots of starch to make the creases sharp. The jeans made the Puma sneakers look so good. Everyone in the group got along and enjoyed getting better together. Then they got the bad news. Rashid and Stephanie told A.D. and the others that they were going to have a baby. They decided to go back home to Jamaica to raise their child. Everyone was happy for them, but they this would mean the end of the Asalaam Brothers and their plan to rise to the top of hip hop culture. Rashid and Stephanie packed their bags and went home in the summertime. A.D. and Donald D talked about all the hard work they had put into building the group. Also, they were disappointed that their music family was broken up. It was a big loss for everyone. Now, they had to find another way to keep improving their hip hop skills on their way to the top. A girl named Kimberly Rodriguez told Donald D that her boyfriend, D.J. Afrika Islam, and his partner, Superman, were looking for MCs for the Funk Machine. She and Donald D were neighbors in the Lambert projects off of Tremont Avenue. The guys decided to try out. After the tryout, A.D. didn't hear back from the group. On his way home from the Boys Club one day, A.D. ran into Gordy B from the group. He thanked A.D. for trying out and told him that they had decided to only pick Donald D. A.D. was very sad, but he had to keep going. He wanted to show them they had made a mistake not to let him join their crew. During the summer, A.D. went to see others groups perform at 63 Park, Arthur Park, the Forest Houses, 118 Park, Bronx River Center, 23 Park, 82 Park, Cedar Park, Forest Park, and St. Mary's Park. There were only a few groups in the world that could draw really big crowds to hip hop events. All of the exciting events were happening in the South Bronx.

D.J. Kool Herc plays with D.J. Clark Kent and MC Coke La Rock at a park jam at 82 Park in the Bronx.

A.D. finally got a chance to see his favorite group. Grandmaster Flash and the Furious Four were playing at Arthur Park. They were amazing. It was a very big park that could hold a lot of people.

The park had ropes around the music crews and their speakers and equipment. It was totally dark except for the lights from the DJs' turntables. The ropes were there to control the crowd and protect the crew and their equipment. Anyone who crossed the ropes would be in big trouble with the crew. This time, there were a few thousand people in the park crowded together for the performance. The peace was shattered when someone shot a gun into the air, and everyone ran in different directions. It was pretty scary and dangerous. This kind of thing happened a lot at music events in the park. It's good that it only caused a big scare and no one was hurt. After the summer, A.D. went to junior high school 136 off Boston Road. He was still writing rhymes and checking out other hip hop groups. His practice and hard work on the court paid off, too, when he made the varsity basketball team. In his freshman year, A.D. found out that Rodney Steve of the Funky Four went to his school and was a grade ahead of him. A.D. was in the seventh grade, and Rodney Steve was in the eighth grade. Also, A.D.'s basketball mate, MC Jazzy Jeff of the Funky Four, went to his school. There were a lot of parties at the Audubon in Harlem. A.D. decided not to go because it was too dangerous. At the time he was too young to go to parties at places like Mitchell Gym and the Black Door. There were lots of places that A.D. couldn't go then because he was still young and couldn't stay out late. In high school, A.D. was still writing his rhymes and building his confidence. Donald D joined the Funk Machine along with Elroy LJ and Kid Vicious. One day, A.D. was sitting in the cafeteria with Cracker Jack, one of the leaders of the Casanovas. He told A.D. that he would get him a tryout with his good friend, Kool DJ AJ. A.D. thought that he had a good chance to be an MC in AJ's group. While A.D. was waiting to be called for the tryout with DJ AJ, he met someone who would change everything.

There was an older kid who sat alone in the cafeteria every day. He put his briefcase on the table and held his head down. He did this for the first few weeks of school. A.D. was curious about this guy and wanted to know who he was. A.D. sat with the other basketball players at a lunch table near the lunchroom door. It was a great spot because they wanted to get their food and sit right down. A.D. asked a guy named Charles to do him a favor. They called him Charlie Rock. He looked just like the guy on the Mad magazine cover, with a missing front tooth and a big grin. A.D. asked Charlie Rock to invite the new guy to sit with them. Charlie brought the new student over, and he introduced himself to everyone at the table. His name was Tony Tone. The guys talked about all kinds of things and made Tony Tone feel welcome. A.D. invited him to hang out with the players at lunchtime instead of sitting alone. A.D. happened to mention that he was an MC.

Easy A.D. and The Original D.J. Tony Tone, Cold Crush Brothers co-founders

Tony Tone let A.D. know that he was forming a group called the Cold Crush Brothers. He told A.D. that since he was an MC, he was automatically down. This was the beginning of the Legendary Cold Crush Brothers. Tony Tone was checking out a Latino brother named Charlie Chase who had very good DJ skills and was with a disco group called Tom and Jerry. Tony went to check out Charlie Chase to see if he was a good fit for the Cold Crush Brothers. Tony Tone finally put together the whole crew. It included Tony Tone, A.D., Charlie Chase, Dota Rock, Whipper Whip, and T-Bone. It was great, but this short-lived version of the group only lasted for about three to six months. This was the first version of the Cold Crush Brothers that most people never heard about. The later Cold Crush Brothers version did some shows around town, including the PAL. They were present at the first-ever MC contest at the PAL. Afrika Bambaataa and other MCs were there working hard for popularity and recognition. The event was attended by Fab Five Freddy and Blondie. They were very well-known performers. This event would become very important in the history of hip hop culture. It was when MCs started showcasing their lyrical ability, and stage presence. They were able to reach a wider audience and launch their careers. The Cold Crush Brothers rehearsed a lot and did some performances in local parks. They were always trying to improve. Without warning, Dota Rock and Whipper Whip left the group. They left to join a more popular hip hop group called the Fantastic Five MCs and D,J. Grand Wizard Theodore. Once again, A.D. was the only MC left. Shortly after Dota Rock and Whipper Whip left, T-Bone just disappeared. The group didn't see him again for many years. The Cold Crush Brothers worked hard to recover from losing so many members. They discussed bringing in additional MCs to strengthen their brand. There was a very good MC that they wanted to join them. His name was Casanova Fly, and he had fantastic skills. He couldn't really show how good he was because the sound system that he used was so bad. It was full of static and not very clear. Tony Tone had an amazing sound system. He had the best speakers and knew exactly how to make performers and their music sound great. Tony Tone invited Casanova Fly to join the group, but he also wanted his partner to join. The rhythmologist Jerry D. Lewis—known as JDL—was Casanova Fly's partner. DJ Charlie Chase didn't think that JDL would be a good choice for the group, but the group overruled him. Casanova Fly and J.D.L both joined the group. D.J. Casanova Fly changed his name to Grand Master Caz. Only two people showed up for the Cold Crush MC tryouts. One was named Dynamite, and the other was Almighty Kay Gee. Kay Gee's voice was close to perfect. He was picked for the final spot. The Cold Crush Brothers were ready to make great music together. They had four MCs: Supreme Easy A.D., Grandmaster Caz, Jerry D. Lewis, and Almighty Kay Gee. There was DJ Charlie Chase and the founder, the original DJ Tony Tone. The group was ready to make an explosion happen—and they did. The Legendary Cold Crush Brothers were on their way to the top of hip hop culture.

Chapter 4

Cold Crush Origins

Back in the day, lots of MCs used to float from group to group. It was hard to stay committed. There were lots of opportunities to try out for a group that more people knew about. The Cold Crush Brothers had their share of people coming and going from the group. Now, they were set with the right MCs and DJs. The group was ready.

The Cold Crush Brothers

South Bronx High School's gym had the regular white backboards. Most schools in the Bronx didn't have the expensive fiberglass backboards. A.D. and the school team wanted to have new backboards and team uniforms, but the school couldn't afford it. A.D. had an idea. He told the coach that the Cold Crush Brothers would throw a dance party in the gym and raise enough money to buy what the team needed. The coach was surprised and not so sure that they could pull it off. A.D. convinced the coach to let the group give it a try.

The Cold Crush Brothers handed out and posted flyers everywhere in the South Bronx community. On the evening of October 17th, it was party time at South Bronx High. The gym was filled with excited guests, and the entire block was packed with people waiting to get in. There was nowhere to move and not enough room inside for even one more person. Some of the people who were waiting to get in became impatient and upset and made bad decisions. They turned over a police car and set it on fire. The police were taken by surprise. They were there to help keep order and to enforce fire department safety rules. Only a certain amount of people were allowed in the gym in order to keep everyone safe. No one anticipated such a large group wanting to see the Cold Crush Brothers. South Bronx High School is located in the heart of the South Bronx.

The Cold Crush Four Mcees - Kay-Gee, Easy A.D. , J.D.L, and Caz at a South Bronx High School party

Most of the crowd outside followed the rules. Unfortunately, it only took a few people to cause a serious problem. The people inside didn't know what was going on outside. The vandals got away, and nobody was hurt. The police cleared the block and sent away everyone who was waiting outside. The dance party was a super success. Everyone inside was safe and had a great time. A.D. and his crew really rocked the party. The Cold Crush 4 MCs—Easy A.D., Almighty Kay Gee, Grand Master Caz, and J.D.L—made enough money to buy two fiberglass backboards. There was also enough to buy shorts and shirts—uniforms for the whole basketball team. A.D. and the team also raised money by selling chocolate bars for one dollar each. A.D. made seven hundred dollars all by himself. The schools bought jackets with the basketball players' names and letters on them. They were unstoppable opponents. The players had the right look as they blew out every opponent. High schools were placed in the A and B division based upon the number of students in a school. The South Bronx High School team won its division on the first try. A banner was hung in their honor in the gym for decades after they had graduated.

South Bronx High School Varsity Basketball Team

The Cold Crush Brothers' popularity grew and grew. When A.D.'s team walked into a gym, someone on the other team would ask if he was Easy A.D. of the Cold Crush Brothers. When he answered yes, they asked if he played ball, too. A.D. always told them to wait and see. Then he and his guys would blow out the other team. A.D.'s team members were Frank Turner, Julio Ortiz, Marvin Coleman, Artie Murphy, Marvin Staton, Claude Stewart, Steven Wilson, David Simmons, and George Ford. Their team had more than just great ball handling and teamwork—they had the best music to win by. The South Bronx High basketball team walked onto the court to the rhythm of "Rock-It In the Pocket" by Fat Beats. The music was strong and clean. It was played by hip hop's first tape master, Elvis Moreno. Some people played basketball, others spit rhymes. Elvis made tapes that were magical, clear and without static. Elvis became the Cold Crush's secret weapon. Some groups had good MCs and DJs, but they didn't have Elvis. Elvis and A.D. met years earlier in the fourth grade. One day, a little chunky boy walked into A.D.'s classroom. Some of the students started laughing and making fun of him. A.D. strongly raised his voice and told the kids to stop laughing at Elvis and to leave him alone. The room went silent. Elvis and A.D. became close friends from that day on. A.D. invited Elvis to record the Cold Crush Brothers' performances. Other groups like Grand Master Flash's and Kool D.J. AJ's and L Brothers performances were great, but their tapes were full of static. It was hard to make out the lyrics clearly or fully enjoy the music. This was because people would put their radios in front of the speakers and record a performance. Then they would come out to the park and play their tape for everyone to hear. Their tapes were full of static. A.D. wanted the Cold Crush tapes to be as clear as possible. DJ Tony Tone showed Elvis how to do it right. He helped Elvis plug straight into the sound system to make the clearest tape possible. This is how Elvis became the first tape master. A.D. and Elvis's friendship and work together would last for decades. Elvis would always be an important part of the Cold Crush Brothers team.

Easy A.D. and Tape Master at Bruckner Flea Market in the Bronx

Elvis's taping process made Cold Crush tapes a great bargain for fans. Most tapes of performances by other artists were full of static. This reduced their listening quality when they were copied. The Cold Crush tapes only lost a little clarity because they were recorded straight from the sound system and then copied. Cold Crush music circulated everywhere because the group was very good, and the tape quality was the best around. People across New York City bought Cold Crush tapes. They enjoyed the music and shared it with their loved ones who lived in other parts of the country, and around the world. Many people shipped Cold Crush tapes to their relatives and friends stationed at military bases in places like Fort Bragg, New Jersey, Rhein-Main Air Base near Frankfurt, Germany, and military bases in Okinawa, Japan. The circulation of Cold Crush Brothers tapes made many new fans for the group in the Army, Air Force, Navy, and Marines. The music spread far and wide to the young people who lived near the military bases and beyond. Easy A.D. saw the school photographer Joey Kane taking pictures of the seniors at the school dance. He invited the photographer to come and take pictures of his group, the Cold Crush Brothers from that point on. Joey Kane became the Cold Crush Brothers' official photographer traveling with the group to every show. Joey Kane changed his name to Joe Conzo in honor of his father. Joe Conzo is officially a Cold Crush Brother and in the history of hip hop is known as the person who has taken hip hop baby pictures. The Cold Crush Brothers took off like a rocket ship. They were on fire. They played lots of cool places including the Audubon Ballroom, Harlem World, the Roxy, Dance Interior, Ecstasy Garage, Cadet Corp, the Cotton Club, the Celebrity Club, the Smith Center, and high school gyms across the city. They became the number-one hip hop group in the country. They had many fans in the U.S., Japan and Europe. Their popularity soared around the same time as the first commercially successful and biggest hip hop record dropped. The record, Rapper's Delight, brought national attention to hip hop for the first time. All eyes were on the Cold Crush Brothers as their performances reached another level. They were excited and ready for the next challenge.

Chapter 5

Battle for Hip Hop Supremacy

On July 3rd in 1981, the Cold Crush 4 battled the Fantastic 5 for hip hop supremacy.

The promotional poster for the Cold Crush Four vs. Fantastic Five Hip Hop Battle at Harlem World, July 3, 1981

Fans from across the city were excited about the big event. At that time, some of the other popular groups had made records and were busy on tour. They were no longer considered to be part of the conversation about hip hop music performances around the city. They were focused on making records and playing for audiences in other parts of the country. The rap game and its style were changing fast. The Cold Crush Brothers was leading the change. The Fantastic 5 crew thought they were unbeatable, but the Cold Crush Brothers knew that they were number one hands down. The Cold Crush Brothers was only in competition with itself. The group's members challenged each other to get better with every rehearsal and performance. Ray Chandler, the manager of Grand Master Flash and the Furious 4 MCs, promoted hip hop shows. Ray was also a friend of the Cold Crush Brothers. He heard excited Cold Crush 4 MCs and the Fantastic 5 MCs' fans debating on the street which group was the best. Ray came up with a bold idea that would alter hip hop history. He arranged a battle for hip hop supremacy between the Cold Crush 4 MCs and the Fantastic 5 and their DJs for a grand prize of $1,000, winner take all. This was a historic moment, and the first battle to take place in the culture of hip hop. The battle would be held at the Harlem World Entertainment Complex, which was one of the most popular places for hip hop music in the city. It was so easy to get to from anywhere in the five boroughs. The fans could quickly reach the complex by subway or car.

The Harlem World building had a massive space with three floors. There was a main floor, an upstairs, and a downstairs. Anyone who couldn't find space on the main floor could watch the show on closed circuit TV on the other floors. The building was packed with excited fans ready to see their group win big. The battle would be decided by the crowd. Whichever crew that the crowd made the most noise for would be the winner. The crews were ready. They had been rivals for a long time, and now it was time to battle. The performances were unbelievable. Both groups showed their fans why they were so popular. The crowd went wild and began screaming and surging towards the stage. When things calmed down, the winner was announced. The crowd had made more noise for the Fantastic 5. They had beaten the Cold Crush Brothers and won the battle for hip hop supremacy. A.D. couldn't believe his ears. He was more than disappointed—he was hurt. His heart and spirit were filled with more pain than he had ever felt in his life.

Easy A.D. takes the stage with his mic in hand at the Harlem World Hip Hop Battle.

Several days later, something amazing surprised the Cold Crush Brothers, the Fantastic 5, their fans, and the hip hop world. The Cold Crush Brothers began circulating a tape of the battle all over the five boroughs for a week after the event was over. Thousands of people who heard the tape in communities across the city chose the Cold Crush Brothers as the true champions of the battle. The Fantastic 5 did not win the battle. The people had spoken. This was a once-in-a- lifetime historic decision by the fans of hip hop music. The Legendary Cold Crush Brothers had won the battle for hip hop supremacy. Now, it was on to the next phase of their journey. From that point on, the Cold Crush Brothers were seen as the masters of hip hop culture. They set new standards for rhyming, style, flows, stage presence, and stage shows. The group traveled across the city to all the boroughs.

Easy A.D. looks ready in his pinstripe suit right before the Battle for Hip Hop Supremacy.

During the Cold Crush's rise to the top, there was a car service called the OJ Car Service. A customer would put a car on hold and rent it for $40 for the whole day. The driver would put on the hottest hip hop tapes for the entire time. OJ Car Service customers were treated to the best hip hop around: tapes of Cold Crush Brothers' performances, along with the music of other popular groups. The Cold Crush tape was the most listened to because of the great music and clear sound. The Cold Crush Brothers were on a roll. They had mastered stage performances, rhyming skills and harmony. They knew how to write smart and long rhymes and mix it together with funky beats. The Cold Crush Brothers also used melodies from familiar songs in pop culture like Harry Chapin's "Cat's in the Cradle," and Paul Simon's "50 Ways to Leave Your Lover," and Barry Manilow's "Copa Cabana." The group was able to use these kinds of songs because of their understanding of pop culture and their mastery of MCing. This is how the Cold Crush Brothers was able to take its music rhyming style to a much higher level well into the future. For years, the Cold Crush Brothers' fans considered the group to be living hip hop legends. The fan excitement led the group to rebrand themselves as the Legendary Cold Crush Brothers. They had finally reached the top. They were now considered the most popular group in hip hop culture.

When the Cold Crush Brothers performed onstage with groups that already had records out, the Cold Crush's performance was the highlight for the fans. When New Edition came out with their first hit, "Candy Girl," they came to New York City to open for the Cold Crush Brothers' shows. The group's manager wanted them to learn how to perform onstage from the best. New Edition played with the Cold Crush at many different places including Harlem World, USA Roller

Skating Rink, and the Empire Roller Skating Rink. Finally, New Edition members were more confident in their stage presence because they had learned from the pros. The Cold Crush Brothers were ready to take their music to new heights.

Chapter 6

Elements - Wild Style Movie

Easy A.D. in the first Hip Hop Movie, Wild Style

Charlie Ahern directed Wild Style along with the assistance of Fab Five Freddy. They wanted to create a movie that showed the elements of hip hop culture. Charlie made a very unusual decision. Instead of having auditions for actors to play the roles of hip hop artists, he got real life hip hop artists to star in the movie. Some special artists and performances were part of the movie. One important scene was the Cold Crush Brothers versus the Fantastic Five in the Basketball Battle. Many years later, this scene was recreated by Sprite. They also reenacted the scene with Little Rodney C and, KK Rockwell of Double Trouble doing a little rhyming on the stoop. This scene was also reenacted years later by Spike Lee, NAS, and AZ. The movie also had a performance by the number-one DJ of all time, Grandmaster Flash. Grandmaster Flash showed his superior skills in the kitchen scene while Fab Five Freddy watched. The B-boys laid down some cardboard and began breakdancing. The great B-boys, Rock Steady and the New York City Breakers, were busting moves. Graffiti artists Lady Pink and Lee Quinones created their exciting graffiti art onscreen. Busy Bee Starski, an artist who always got the party started, was also in the movie. Wild Style showed the audiences what was happening in hip hop culture at that time. The idea to use the original artists as cast members was a very smart choice. It gave the movie a special kind of energy that made it feel like real life. Wild Style was shot in 1981, finished in 1982, and shown in theaters in 1983. The soon-to-become-classic hip hop feature-length film premiered in Times Square. It broke screening records by selling out at all screenings in its three-week run. The film was later released on home video in 1997 and on DVD for its twenty-fifth anniversary. Also, a thirty-year special edition for collectors was released on Blu-ray in 2012. This exciting and historic movie continued to influence hip hop culture for many decades. The movie was first shown at a 42nd Street theater in Manhattan, New York City. It was a big piece of history because it was the first hip hop movie ever made. The critics gave it good reviews, which made the producers, artists and fans very happy. The artists in the movie were able to do something that was a first for hip hop artists. They were able to show movie audiences the amazing elements of hip hop. The elements are MCing, DJing, graffiti, and breakdancing. These elements made up the rhymes, music, moves, and styles that no one had ever seen on-screen before.

After the movie was released in New York City, it went across the country and around the world. It was seen in many different cities and countries. Some audiences had heard the music before, and others were new to hip hop. This was the first time that so many people were getting to see all the elements of hip hop culture up close. Then something even more exciting happened. The Wild Style tour team collaborated with an amazing Japanese supporter of hip hop. Katsusuke Kuzui was a visionary promoter who worked in New York City and Japan. He produced the publicity for the first public release of Wild Style in Japan. Katsusuke helped generate enthusiasm for the growth of the country's hip hop scene. This new cultural phenomenon launched from the South Bronx to venues in Japan to cities across the globe. Hip hop was on its way to becoming an unstoppable cultural force.

In 1983, the Cold Crush Brothers, along with a group of twenty-two other hip hop artists and DJs and MCs, graffiti artists, breakdancers, left for an adventure in Tokyo and Osaka, Japan. They were going on a historic tour to perform and share hip hop culture with young people 6,916 miles away. The tour took place at the same time the movie was released in local theaters. The tour plan was to screen the film at several locations, followed by a live performances. It was time to make new friends and fans. Japanese youth were about to join a cultural revolution that started in the South Bronx. They would soon help the Wild Style artists share hip hop culture with people across the globe.

After being greeted by an enthusiastic crowd at the airport, the artists arrived at a very nice hotel. The group members performed at many movie theaters in the cities of Tokyo and Osaka. After one of the shows, the entire group went to perform at Seibu Department Store in Tokyo, one of the largest in the world. It was an exciting and unusual experience for the group to perform in such a venue. It was big enough to hold different kinds of events at the same time. The shoppers and fans were thrilled to see the Cold Crush Brothers perform. It was a once-in-a-lifetime experience for them and for the artists, too. The Cold Crush Brothers were so excited to ride the bullet train, the fastest train in the world. They also performed at parks and other venues around the two cities. In those days, Japanese young people were big fans of Elvis Presley. They had a special park where fans came every Sunday to have fun and dress up like Elvis.. Things had changed by the time the Wild Style tour was over. Many fans in the park were dressing like B-boys and B-girls. Something beautiful and important happened. The Wild Style tour and its artists brought hip hop culture to Japan, and it never left. It grew and remained an important part of Japanese youth culture for decades. It also helped inspire young people from many other countries to experience and enjoy the culture, too.

Wild Style was a low-budget independent movie. It didn't cost much to make, and it didn't make lots of money like popular blockbuster films. It wasn't connected to a big film company with famous stars like lots of other movies. It had something very different and original. The movie made a very big impact because its performers weren't actors. They were the real deal. They didn't have to pretend or copy anything. They were the original creators of their art. It was something very exciting that people wanted to experience and be part of. Wild Style was the first hip hop movie in the world. There can only be one first. Many people saw the movie when it was released in Japan. Some were in the audience at the theaters where the Cold Crush performed after the film was shown. Others saw the movie before the group arrived in the country. Many people had a chance to meet the artists in-person at a show or at a club. It didn't matter how or when they first heard the music. The new fans loved it and couldn't get enough. There was an instant connection between the Cold Crush Brothers and their fans. The group gave fans a new way of expressing themselves as young people living in a very formal society. It was nothing like their experience as fans of pop stars like Elvis. Hip hop culture was a new kind of music and experience, with exciting elements to explore and express in their own way. It was a special gift given by new friends from the other side of the world.

There is a kind of magic between the tour's artists and their fans during a performance. It didn't matter that the audience didn't speak the language of the music. They easily learned to recite the rhymes and lyrics of the songs and connected to the artists' messages. In just a few weeks, the Wild Style artists were able to share the elements of hip hop culture with their Japanese fans.

From that point on, Japanese society was changed forever. Japan has an amazing culture that has lasted for thousands of years and influenced other people from around the world. After their Wild Style experience, many Japanese youth would make the elements of hip hop their own. The Wild Style movie brought hip hop to many countries. Cold Crush Brothers' fans from many places already knew and loved their music. Lots of U.S. fans had shared performance tapes with their friends and relatives at various military bases. They were very excited to see the movie. Wild Style helped hip hop culture grow throughout the towns and cities of places far away from the South Bronx, where it began. There were many hip hop movies that came later. None of the films that followed could equal the impact of Wild Style on youth culture worldwide. A.D. and the Cold Crush Brothers had their Wild Style scenes shot at various locations in the South Bronx and Manhattan. The basketball scene was shot on 181st Street in a schoolyard. The battle between the Cold Crush Brothers and the Fantastic Five was held at the Dixie. The group performed at the Lower East Side Bandshell where the final scene of the movie was shot. A.D. and the group worked hard but they also had lots of fun. Their adventure in Japan was captured in books, magazines, newspapers, television, and radio. They were interviewed on a big television show by Tamari, the country's top comedian. He helped his guests relax and enjoy some laughs with the audience.

When they weren't rehearsing and performing, the Cold Crush Brothers enjoyed the people they met and learned a lot about Japanese culture. They tried their best to make every performance better than the one before. The tour schedule was tough, but the group members were young and strong. They were able to get a little rest between performances and appearances and then get right back to work. All of the Cold Crush Brothers didn't make the tour. Tony Tone, Easy A.D., Almighty Kay Gee, and Charlie Chase made it. Unfortunately, JDL was afraid of flying and stayed home. Flying across the world was a pretty scary thing, especially for someone who was very afraid of flying. The guys in the group missed JDL, but they had to keep things moving. There wasn't any time to feel sad. Some members of the group experienced their first plane ride. It was a straight flight from New York to Tokyo for fourteen very long hours. It was quite an adventure for everyone.

The trip to the airport was like something out of a movie. It was early in the morning on a very hot day. A.D. came out of the building and down the stairs carrying his bags. There was only one car on the side of the street. It was a black limousine parked and quietly waiting for A.D. The street was clear because the street sweeper hadn't arrived yet. The limousine was picking up everyone in the group at their home. A.D.'s parents and sisters were looking out of the windows. They were so proud and excited to see A.D. go off on his adventure. A.D. was filled with emotion. He wasn't sure exactly how he was supposed to feel. He was happy, excited, sad, and a little scared. He had never been away from his family and friends. The South Bronx was the only world that he knew and loved. Now, he was leaving it to fly off to a strange place. Even though he would miss his family and home, he felt strong and ready. A.D. stepped into the limousine, and the next level of his quest began. Getting ready for the trip was a new experience. All of the group's members had to get passports and work visas. These were things that none of them knew anything about. The organizers of the tour helped everyone get the necessary paperwork on time. The tour planners took care of everything successfully. It took a lot of focus and coordination to make the travel arrangements for the group The Cold Crush Brothers and the other Wild Style cast members were excited and relieved when the plane landed at the Tokyo, Japan, airport. The trip was long, and they were all tired. As they walked from the plane to the airport, they noticed something a little odd. They were surprised and excited to see that so many things were automated. Most of the doors opened without being touched. There were very cool things to buy—bullet train clocks, cartoon characters, Coke signs written in English and Japanese, Voltron robots, and many other cool space-age things to see. Their walk through the super-clean airport felt like they had entered the world of the Jetsons, with lots of advanced technology in the year 1983.

The group had an amazing time at the President Hotel. Everyone on the tour was given a $50 daily advance to use for everyday extra things. They all had meal vouchers to get free breakfast, lunch, and dinner. The food was delicious, and the staff worked hard to make everything perfect. A.D. was always the first up in the morning to go downstairs to breakfast while the others slept late. All of the hotel guests were Japanese, except for the Wild Style tour group. They were the only Black and brown people that they saw in the hotel or anywhere else. It really didn't matter because they felt very special. The group was treated like stars by the staff and the other hotel guests. The tour was announced on television and in the news, and everyone gave them lots of Wherever they went, people smiled and waved. They felt like real stars. The food was good and very much like American food, except it seemed fresher. They had all of the brands that A.D. and the tour artists were used to buying. They had Coca-Cola, Wendy's, Kentucky Fried Chicken, potato chips, ice cream, and all the other stuff that was popular back home. There was always too much food. When the group had some free time, their guide and translator would take them out in a shuttle bus to visit fun places in town. Each time they got back on the bus after a visit, fresh snacks were waiting for them. The group was driven to performances and appearances by a chauffeur. The people in Japan were not used to seeing so many Black and brown people, except when the U.S. sailors were in town. The Navy ships were still out to sea and didn't return until after the tour. The sailors were treated like special people, and so were the tour's artists. A.D. felt very happy to be on his big adventure in Japan. A.D. thought it was something that was supposed to happen.

A.D. loved the way Japanese people treated everyone in the tour group. They were very respectful and caring. He appreciated their customs and the way they greeted and cared for people they didn't even know. It was a real culture shock to be greeted so warmly. The hotel and tour support staff gave the group lots of attention and made sure that they had everything they needed. A.D. was impressed by the respect the people had for each other and for their elders and visitors to their country. It was great to feel welcome and comfortable. It was a chance to experience a new and exciting culture. A.D. and the group were comfortable mingling with the people and having laughs and signing autographs. It was so enjoyable to be appreciated and treated special. A.D. felt embraced by the whole country. It was more than just having lots of new fans. It was as though the people of Japan were happy to accept and respect hip hop culture even though it was new and very different from what they were used to.

As a young man who wasn't even twenty years old yet, A.D. was very appreciative. He was a minority kid from the South Bronx who had traveled out of his home city for the first time. He was co-starring in a major groundbreaking movie that was going to put hip hop culture on the map. He was on tour with other artists in an exciting country thousands of miles from home performing for amazing new fans. A.D. knew that his experience in Japan would change the way he saw things forever. It would also change the young people of Japan. The tour would leave a slice of hip hop culture with them to grow and make their own in the future. The impact of the Wild Style tour would be amazing and everlasting for the artists, and for the young people of Japan, too. The language barrier wasn't really a big deal. The group had a very good translator, and there were a few other people on the tour support team who also spoke English. The translator was important for television and magazine interviews, store signings, and question-and-answer sessions after performances. The best way to communicate with fans and other people was through body language and simple gestures. Some people knew basic English phrases, and the tour group learned a few words in Japanese. It was fun learning to speak in new ways. Communicating through music was the easy part.

The performances at the various venues went smoothly. The Japanese production crew took care of everything. The tour group members only had to bring their own turntables and music. The group toured different theaters and clubs around the city. The group would perform right after the movie was shown. Then there would be a question-and-answer session. The production crew always made sure that the sound system and everything else was always in place. They ran a smooth operation. A.D. felt like the Cold Crush Brothers' rise to the top of hip hop was a natural thing. It seemed like it was supposed to happen. Being part of the movie was big accomplishment for the group. The difference was now everyone knew who they were, because their names and faces were everywhere. Their music was familiar to many more people because they were in a major movie. In addition to co-starring in the movie, their original music from their past performances was included on the soundtrack.

The group was having fun doing what they were meant to do and getting paid a bit more for it. It was a fantastic feeling. This is what each member of the Cold Crush Brothers had been working so hard for over the years. The movie and the tour were both important firsts. A.D. and the Cold Crush Brothers had come a very long way. They started out as separate young artists trying to find their way in a new industry. There was no blueprint to follow, since everything was new. All of the other hip hop artists were trying to find their way, too. Once A.D. started his music journey, he saw a lot of MCs and DJs come and go. He finally joined with DJ Tony Tone to create the Legendary Cold Crush Brothers. After lots of ups and downs, they finally came together as a group ready to work their way to the top. It seemed like it was their destiny.

Chapter 7

From Cassette Tapes to Records

Initially, making records was very foreign to the Cold Crush Brothers. The group was from the beginning of hip hop, where street credibility meant everything. In the summertime they played

Easy A.D. and the Cold Crush Brothers onstage

outside in the parks. In the winter they played inside various venues and charged money to see the show. That was how groups built their brands back in the day. The group sold lots of cassette tapes citywide, nationally, and globally. The Cold Crush Brothers made and marketed their own music, and they were in charge of the process.

The Cold Crush Brothers started making records because many of their colleagues were making records, and they decided that they needed to be in the mix. Their first record was Weekend, released in 1982 on the Elite Records label. It was about the days of the week, and the regular things that kids and their parents would do to enjoy the weekend. Weekend was the Cold Crush's first record, and it turned out to be an exciting experience. They all had lots of fun sitting in the recording booth, learning to handle the microphones and headphones.

The Cold Crush's next record experience was making new material for the soundtrack of the movie Wild Style. The producers took several scenes and put their new music over them to be used as singles on the soundtrack. This was another fun learning adventure. The group was proud and excited to be on the first hip hop soundtrack ever.

Their third record was Punk Rock Rap. During this period, hip hop had moved its roots from the Bronx and the other boroughs to downtown Manhattan and the Village. For the first time, the group spent money on live musicians playing keyboards. The group fused rock and hip hop together and created hip hop rap. That was the first time that any group had merged the two types of music. It set the standard for other hip hop artists in the future.

Punk Rock Rap was released on the CBS Records label through Tuff City in 1983. The Cold Crush Brothers was the first group to be signed by a subsidiary label which was handled by their management company, Tuff City. Unfortunately, the management company did not look out for the financial interests of the Cold Crush members.

The Cold Crush Brothers were trusting and naive young men who knew nothing about the cutthroat way the music business operated. Just like them, many young artists from Black and brown communities were taken advantage of financially by selfish and greedy music executives. It was a painful and costly learning experience for the group.

The music executives at CBS Records were surprised when they met the members of the Cold Crush Brothers. Before the meeting, they mistakenly thought that the group was white instead of Black.

They had problems figuring out the best ways to market the song. Punk Rock Rap did very well with the white fan base, and not so well among non-fans. It was like a glimpse into the future, where young white fans would buy more hip hop music than any other group. Finally, the Cold Crush Brothers returned to their musical roots and released Fresh Wild Fly and Bold. The song was a reminder of the group's origin and its place in hip hop culture. It was released on Profile Records in 1984. The record sold 16,000 units in one week. This was a big deal at the time. Sadly, the executives from Profile Records and Tuff City had a big dispute about the record profits. They both refused to compromise and make a deal. Profile Records was a much bigger label and distribution company. Profile cut ties with Tuff City and the Cold Crush Brothers. This left all of the record pressing up to Tuff City, and it was not up to the job.

As a result of the poor choices and greedy actions by the record companies involved, the Cold Crush Brothers' records never reached commercial success. Although the group did continue making records, the ones they did make are very important. Weekend, Punk Rock Rap, Fresh Wild Fly, and Bold are essential parts of the group's amazing journey from shows in New York City parks to stage performances in Japan. Their records represent a rung in the group's historic climb up the ladder of hip hop culture. The group was made up of young aspiring artists from a South Bronx neighborhood. They dared to cut a musical path to the future, leaving clear markers for others to follow. The Legendary Cold Crush Brothers' music—rhythm, flow, lyrics, style, confidence, and stage presence—are now an important part of hip hop culture's historic rise. The group has earned its rightful place alongside some of the most iconic artists of hip hop culture as it nears its fiftieth anniversary. Stay tuned for more untold stories about hip hop pioneers.

Featured Track

Freestyle

Supreme Easy A.D.
Freestyle
My goal is the same, I aim for fame
I don't pop no game (He don't have no dame)
Never put to shame because I have a brain
Supreme Easy A.D. is the name that I claim
Never brag about my crew but you know what we can do
Don't have no LP, but we're not blue
Our rhymes are the tools to set the mood

If you won't bother us, we won't bother you
We're the Cold Crush crew, that's what I said
All you wack MCs, get it through your heads
As you listen to me speak as I reach my peak
Because I never bite a rhyme, I never repeat
Because I'm Easy A, going all the way
Keeping up the funky pace to the break of day
And then you get up, a-then ya get down
(And rock) And rock to (And rock and rock) and rock to the beat
Supreme Easy rock all you need
You rock to the beat 'cause I'm so sweet
I'm guaranteed to rock the house and get you out of your seat
Well I'm Supreme A.D. as you can trust
Rockin' to the funky beat I'm the serious must
I'm down with the four, I'm down with the four
I'm down with the four known as the Cold Crush
The Cold Crush crew (The what?)
The Cold Crush crew (Say what?)
Is guaranteed to get the party people in the groove (Say what?)
Cold Crush crew got nothin' to prove
But rock the house for you and you
And Kay Gee (Ha ha), Kay Gee (Ha ha)
Kay Gee (Ha ha), Kay Gee (Ha ha)
Kay Gee (Ha hoo), my throat is sore
Homeboy, get on the mic, get on the mic goddammit
Get on the mic with your rhymes galore.

Epilogue

A Message From A.D.

"The first book in our book series, Easy A.D., is the story of my life growing up in the South Bronx, one of the most beautiful spaces on the planet.

Young Easy A.D.

My amazing journey took me through the exciting birth of hip hop in 1973, the destructive burning of the South Bronx during the 1970s, and the life-changing New York City blackout of 1977. I believe that destiny led me to a place where my love for music and sports would come together: the Hoe Avenue Boys & Girls Club in the South Bronx. My skills as a hip hop MC were grown like planted seeds at different venues across the city, and eventually, on stages abroad. My crew and I played in the warm weather at outdoor city park jams at 63 Park, Arthur Park, 82 Park, Cedar Park, and many more spaces. We moved our performances indoors when the weather got colder. We played at the Dixie Club,

Ecstasy Garage, and many high school gyms and community centers. We perfected our music lyrics and stage presence as we moved from playing local city venues to performing for audiences 6,739 miles away in Japan. We helped spread the love of hip hop music to young people throughout New York City's boroughs, around the country, and across the globe, where it would grow for almost fifty years. Hip hop is a dynamic culture that brings people together. The music is the vibration of the lives of the individuals who create it. Along with my peers in the culture, I grew up in a world that had no fear. We dared to pull from the things that were happening all around us and fused them into a powerful and unique culture that would help shape the future.

I present to you, some of my life stories. As they say in Japanese, Arigatou (thank you). Watashi ha Tokyo ga suki (I love Tokyo).

Easy A.D., a true hip hop pioneer.

Acknowledgments

This children's book wouldn't be happening without my partner, Charles Taylor Jr., and the support of my Cold Crush Brothers, in particular, one Cold Crush Brother, the Original D.J. Tony Tone, and my friends in life, my Tape Master and Joe Conzo Jr. We made history together, and this story belongs to all of us.

I've got to give honor and respect to my mother, who never told me no at anytime in my life, and my father who helped bring me to this planet.

Also, I give much honor and respect to my hip hop brother DMC for always being present and for his kind words.

I give much appreciation to all the hip hop practitioners and educators, and lovers of hip hop, who keep moving the culture forward. I would be remiss not to mention all the MCees, DJs, graffiti writers, breakdancers, music producers, and fashion designers - keeping the art form present. Thank you all for helping to make something so amazing that the world has fallen in love with it.

Whether you're in the Bronx or on the other side of the world, I hope my story and the stories in this book series inspire you to find your own voice and make your mark.

Peace, love, honor and respect.
Easy A.D.

www.ingramcontent.com/pod-product-compliance
Lightning Source LLC
Chambersburg PA
CBHW032100150426
43194CB00006B/591